THE
JAMES DARREN
STORY

From Teen Idol to Timeless Talent

By Joel Lauzon

Table Of Contents

Introduction

Overview of a Multifaceted Career

James Darren's life and career reflect the story of a man who was more than just a teen idol. He was a talented actor, singer, and director who left an indelible mark on the entertainment industry. Darren's journey from the streets of Philadelphia to the heights of Hollywood success is one of perseverance, talent, and a constant drive to reinvent himself. This book aims to explore the many facets of James Darren's life, from his humble beginnings to his lasting legacy, while honoring his contributions to film, television, and music.

Born James William Ercolani on June 8, 1936, in Philadelphia, Darren's early years were shaped by the vibrant culture of his Italian-American neighborhood. He was raised in a working-class family that instilled in him the values of hard work and determination, which would later guide him through the unpredictable world of show business. Philadelphia, with its rich history and diverse population, provided a fertile ground for Darren's early artistic inclinations. It was here that he first dreamed of a life beyond the ordinary, captivated by the allure of cinema and the glamor of Hollywood.

Darren's path to stardom was not a straight line. His early years were marked by struggles and setbacks, but also by moments of inspiration that pushed him to pursue his dreams. This chapter delves into those formative years, exploring how his upbringing in Philadelphia influenced his career and shaped the man he would become. It was in these early days that Darren developed a love for performance, a passion that would carry him through decades of success in an industry known for its fickleness.

The Early Years in Philadelphia

James Darren's story begins in the tight-knit community of South Philadelphia, where he grew up surrounded by the rich traditions of his Italian heritage. His parents, who were hardworking and dedicated, encouraged him to follow his passions, even if those passions led him far from the expected paths of the time. Darren was a curious and ambitious child, always eager to learn and explore new avenues, whether in school, on the streets, or at home. His natural charm and charisma made him a popular figure among his peers, and it wasn't long before he discovered a love for performing.

The cultural landscape of Philadelphia in the 1940s and 1950s was vibrant and diverse, offering young Darren exposure to various forms of entertainment, from the lively music scene to the burgeoning film industry. It was during this time that Darren first began to dream of a career in Hollywood. He was captivated by the movies he saw at the local theaters, and he knew that he wanted to be a part of that world. However, breaking into the entertainment industry was no easy feat, especially for a young boy from a working-class background.

Despite the challenges, Darren was determined to pursue his dream. He started by performing in school plays and local talent shows, where his natural abilities quickly became apparent.

His performances were marked by a sincerity and passion that set him apart from others. It was clear that Darren had a gift, and those around him encouraged him to take his talents to the next level. The early years in Philadelphia were not just a time of discovery for Darren, but also a time of preparation, as he honed his skills and built the foundation for a career that would eventually take him to Hollywood.

The Journey to Hollywood: From New York to the Silver Screen

James Darren's journey to Hollywood was a testament to his determination and resilience. After leaving Philadelphia, Darren moved to New York City, where he hoped to find more opportunities to pursue his acting career. New York was the hub of the entertainment world at the time, offering aspiring actors the chance to train with some of the best in the business. Darren enrolled at the Stella Adler Studio of Acting, where he studied under the legendary Stella Adler herself. It was here that he began to develop the skills that would define his career.

Studying with Adler was a transformative experience for Darren. She instilled in him a deep respect for the craft of acting and taught him the importance of discipline, focus, and emotional honesty. These lessons would stay with Darren throughout his career, influencing not only his performances but also his approach to life. In New York, Darren faced the challenges that all aspiring actors encounter—auditions, rejections, and the constant pressure to prove himself. However, his talent and persistence eventually paid off.

Darren's big break came when he was signed by Columbia Pictures in the late 1950s. His first major role was in the film *Rumble on the Docks* (1956), a gritty drama that showcased Darren's ability to portray complex characters. This role opened doors for Darren, leading to more opportunities in Hollywood. Soon after, he was cast in the role that would change his life forever—Moondoggie in the 1959 film *Gidget*. This role catapulted Darren to stardom, making him a household name and solidifying his status as a teen idol. The journey from

Philadelphia to Hollywood was complete, but Darren's career was just beginning.

The Enduring Appeal of James Darren

James Darren's appeal extended far beyond his roles as a teen idol. While he became famous for his work in films like *Gidget*, his career was marked by a versatility that allowed him to transcend the limitations of typecasting. Darren was not content to be defined by a single role or genre; instead, he sought out opportunities to challenge himself and grow as an artist. This drive for constant reinvention is one of the reasons why Darren's career endured for so many decades.

Darren's ability to connect with audiences on a deep, emotional level was one of his greatest strengths. Whether he was playing the carefree Moondoggie or the sophisticated Vic Fontaine on *Star Trek: Deep Space Nine*, Darren brought a sense of authenticity to his roles that resonated with viewers. His performances were always grounded in a genuine understanding of the characters he portrayed, and this sincerity made him a beloved figure in both film and television.

Moreover, Darren's career was not limited to acting. He was also a successful singer and director, further showcasing his versatility and talent. His music career, which included hits like "Goodbye Cruel World," added another dimension to his appeal, allowing him to reach audiences through multiple mediums. As a director, Darren brought his experience and understanding of the industry to bear, contributing to the success of shows like *T.J. Hooker* and *Beverly Hills, 90210*. The enduring appeal of James Darren lies in his ability to adapt and evolve, always staying relevant in an ever-changing industry.

Setting the Stage: Why This Book Matters

This book is more than just a biography; it is a tribute to a man who touched the lives of millions through his work in film, television, and music. James Darren's career spanned more than five decades, during which he left an indelible mark on popular culture. From his early days as a teen idol to his later work as an actor, singer, and director, Darren's story is one of resilience, talent, and a deep love for his craft.

In writing this book, the goal is not only to celebrate Darren's achievements but also to explore the man behind the roles. What drove him to pursue such a varied and successful career? How did he navigate the challenges of fame and the pressures of the entertainment industry? And what is the legacy that he leaves behind? These are the questions that this book seeks to answer, offering readers a comprehensive and empathetic look at the life of James Darren.

In addition to honoring Darren's memory, this book also serves as a reminder of the impact that one person can have on the world. Darren's work continues to inspire new generations of actors, musicians, and fans, and his legacy will undoubtedly endure for years to come. By documenting his life and career, this book aims to preserve that legacy and ensure that James

Darren's contributions to the entertainment industry are remembered and celebrated.

The Rise of a Teen Idol

Early Life and Influences

James Darren's early life laid the foundation for the multifaceted career that would follow. Born into a working-class Italian-American family in South Philadelphia, Darren was shaped by the vibrant cultural heritage of his neighborhood. His upbringing was filled with the sounds, flavors, and stories that come with being part of a close-knit immigrant community, and his family played an integral role in nurturing his ambitions. His parents, who valued hard work and perseverance, supported his creative pursuits, even though they may not have fully understood the depth of his artistic dreams at the time.

Growing up, Darren's life was filled with typical childhood experiences, but there was always something special about him. His magnetic personality and natural charm made him a standout among his peers, but it was his passion for performance that truly set him apart. Influenced by the movies he watched in the local theaters and the music that filled the streets, Darren's love for acting and singing was ignited early. Whether mimicking scenes from the silver screen or performing impromptu songs for friends and family, it was clear that he was destined for something more than the ordinary life his community often expected.

From the beginning, family and community played crucial roles in shaping Darren's identity. The values he learned at home—respect, humility, and determination—would become the guiding principles throughout his career. These early influences not only provided him with a strong sense of self but also gave him the resilience needed to navigate the challenging path to stardom. Darren's early aspirations, though ambitious, were rooted in the authenticity of his upbringing. He didn't just want fame—he wanted to make his family proud and show that someone from a small neighborhood in Philadelphia could achieve greatness on the biggest stages.

Breaking into Hollywood

James Darren's journey to Hollywood began with a deep commitment to his craft, something that became evident during his studies with the renowned acting coach Stella Adler in New York City. Adler was known for her emphasis on emotional authenticity and artistic integrity, and her teachings had a profound impact on Darren. Under Adler's guidance, he developed a deep understanding of the art of acting, learning to channel his emotions and bring authenticity to every role. This period of intense study would prove to be instrumental in shaping Darren's approach to acting, providing him with the tools needed to stand out in a competitive industry.

Darren's first roles were modest, but they showcased his talent and potential. His debut in *Rumble on the Docks* (1956) demonstrated his ability to portray complex characters, and it wasn't long before Hollywood took notice. Signing with Columbia Pictures was a turning point in his career, as it allowed Darren to break into the mainstream and take on more prominent roles. However, the road to success was far from easy. The entertainment industry was notoriously difficult to break into, especially for young actors, but Darren's persistence and talent helped him overcome the initial challenges.

His early successes in Hollywood weren't just the result of good luck. Darren was strategic in his choices, opting for roles that showcased his range and allowed him to grow as an actor. He understood the importance of building a strong foundation in his career, and each role was a stepping stone toward his eventual stardom. Though the journey was fraught with uncertainties, Darren's dedication to his craft and his belief in his abilities ensured that he was always moving forward.

The 'Gidget' Phenomenon

The defining moment of James Darren's career came when he was cast as Moondoggie in the 1959 film *Gidget*. This role would catapult him into the spotlight, transforming him into a teen idol and solidifying his place in popular culture. The movie, which starred Sandra Dee as the titular character, became an instant hit, capturing the imagination of audiences across America. *Gidget* was more than just a teen romance; it was a cultural touchstone that reflected the carefree spirit of youth and the emerging surf culture of the time.

For Darren, landing the role of Moondoggie was a life-changing event. It wasn't just that the movie was successful—it was that Moondoggie became a symbol of youthful freedom and adventure. Darren's portrayal of the charming and easygoing surfer boy resonated with audiences, making him a heartthrob overnight. His ability to embody the character so effortlessly endeared him to fans, who saw in him the ideal of the perfect boyfriend—handsome, kind, and just a little bit rebellious.

The cultural impact of *Gidget* extended far beyond the screen. The film helped to popularize surfing as a mainstream activity and contributed to the development of the "beach movie" genre that would dominate the 1960s. Darren, as the face of this movement, became an icon of the era. However, with instant stardom came the pressures of fame. Darren had to navigate the challenges of being a public figure, dealing with the intense scrutiny that accompanied his new celebrity status. Though he embraced the opportunities that *Gidget* afforded him, Darren was also mindful of the typecasting that often came with such iconic roles.

Balancing Acting and Music

In addition to his success as an actor, James Darren also made a name for himself in the music industry. His role in *Gidget* not only showcased his acting talent but also his musical abilities. Darren performed the movie's theme song, which became a hit in its own right, further establishing him as a multi-talented performer. Singing came naturally to Darren, and his smooth, velvety voice quickly won over fans who admired his versatility. It was clear that Darren wasn't just a one-dimensional teen idol—he was a true entertainer.

Following the success of the *Gidget* theme song, Darren launched a successful music career, releasing a string of hits in the early

1960s. His song "Goodbye Cruel World" became a chart-topping single, earning him a gold record and solidifying his status as a pop sensation. Darren's ability to seamlessly transition between acting and music set him apart from many of his peers, and he quickly became one of the most sought-after performers of his time.

However, balancing two careers was no easy feat. Darren had to manage the demands of both Hollywood and the recording studio, often juggling acting roles with music tours and performances. Despite the challenges, Darren excelled in both fields, proving that he was more than capable of handling the pressures that came with being a dual-threat entertainer. His success in both acting and music ensured that Darren's star would continue to rise, allowing him to forge a lasting career that spanned multiple decades and mediums.

Beyond Gidget: The Struggle for Identity

Avoiding Typecasting

James Darren's success as Moondoggie in *Gidget* was both a blessing and a curse. While the role catapulted him to fame, it also threatened to pigeonhole him as the quintessential teen heartthrob, making it difficult for him to be seen as anything else. Darren reprised his iconic role in the sequels *Gidget Goes Hawaiian* (1961) and *Gidget Goes to Rome* (1963), but by this point, he was beginning to feel the strain of being forever linked to a single character. These roles, though commercially successful, reinforced the public's perception of Darren as Moondoggie, a persona that, while beloved, did not fully represent his range as an actor.

The struggle with typecasting was a significant challenge for Darren. As much as he appreciated the opportunities that *Gidget* had provided, he was keenly aware of the limitations it imposed on his career. Being seen primarily as Moondoggie meant that Darren had to work twice as hard to convince casting directors and audiences that he was capable of more complex, diverse roles. This struggle was not just professional but personal, as Darren wrestled with the desire to be recognized for his full artistic potential rather than just his youthful charm.

In response to this challenge, Darren made deliberate choices to break away from the Moondoggie mold. He began seeking out roles that allowed him to explore different facets of his talent, even if it meant taking on smaller or less glamorous parts. This strategic approach was not without its risks, but it was necessary for Darren to carve out a new identity in Hollywood. By diversifying his roles, he slowly began to redefine himself, proving that he was more than just a teen idol.

A Journey into Television

As Darren sought to broaden his career, television emerged as a viable platform for reinvention. The shift from the big screen to the small screen marked a new chapter in his career, one that allowed him to explore a wider array of characters and storylines. His role in the science fiction series *The Time Tunnel* (1966-1967) was a significant departure from his previous work. In this series, Darren played Tony Newman, a scientist who becomes trapped in a time-travel experiment gone awry. The show's blend of historical adventure and futuristic technology provided Darren with an opportunity to showcase his versatility as an actor.

The Time Tunnel was just the beginning of Darren's foray into television. Throughout the 1970s and 1980s, he made guest appearances on numerous iconic TV shows, including *Love, American Style*, *Fantasy Island*, and *The Love Boat*. Each appearance allowed Darren to demonstrate his range, from romantic leads to more nuanced, dramatic roles. These guest spots were crucial in helping him shed the Moondoggie image, allowing audiences to see him in a variety of lights.

Reinvention, however, was not without its challenges. The television landscape was competitive, and Darren had to continuously prove himself in an industry that often favored younger, fresher faces. Despite these obstacles, Darren's determination and talent ensured that he remained a relevant and respected figure in Hollywood. His ability to adapt to the changing demands of the industry highlighted his resilience and his unwavering commitment to his craft.

European Sojourn

In the late 1960s, James Darren took a bold step in his career by accepting a role in the Italian film *Venus in Furs* (1969), directed by the infamous Jess Franco. This move to Europe was driven by a desire to escape the constraints of Hollywood typecasting and to explore new creative opportunities. Working abroad offered Darren a chance to reinvent himself artistically, away from the familiar pressures of the American entertainment industry.

Venus in Furs was a psychological thriller that was markedly different from the roles Darren had previously undertaken. The film's surreal, avant-garde style and its darker themes were a significant departure from the wholesome, youthful characters he had portrayed in the past. Darren's performance in the film was critically acclaimed, proving that he was capable of handling complex and challenging material. The experience of working in Europe also gave Darren a fresh perspective on his career, allowing him to return to the United States with renewed confidence and a broader artistic vision.

Darren's time in Europe was brief but impactful. After his stint abroad, he returned to American television, where he continued to build on the momentum he had gained from his European experience. This period of his career was characterized by a newfound depth in his performances, as he drew on the lessons learned from working in a different cultural and cinematic environment. His European sojourn was a key moment in his ongoing struggle to break free from typecasting, further solidifying his status as a versatile and talented actor.

The Role of Vic Fontaine

In 1998, James Darren found himself once again in the spotlight with his role as Vic Fontaine in *Star Trek: Deep Space Nine*. Fontaine, a holographic lounge singer, was a character that seemed tailor-made for Darren, blending his acting and musical talents in a way that resonated deeply with both old fans and a new generation of viewers. The role was a significant departure from his earlier work, allowing Darren to explore a character that was not only charming and charismatic but also wise and reflective.

Vic Fontaine was more than just a lounge singer; he was a confidant and advisor to the crew of Deep Space Nine, often providing sage advice and emotional support to characters grappling with complex issues. Darren's portrayal of Fontaine was imbued with a warmth and sincerity that made the character beloved by fans. The role allowed Darren to draw on his own life experiences, infusing Fontaine with a sense of lived wisdom and authenticity.

The success of Vic Fontaine also marked a resurgence in Darren's career, introducing him to a new audience while reconnecting him with longtime fans. The character's popularity demonstrated that Darren's appeal transcended generations, proving that he was more than capable of adapting to the evolving landscape of television. Vic Fontaine became a cultural touchstone in its own right, and Darren's portrayal of the character remains one of the most memorable aspects of *Deep Space Nine*. Through Fontaine, Darren was able to fully integrate his dual talents as an actor and singer, showcasing the enduring versatility that had defined his career for decades.

The Director's Chair

Transitioning to Directing

As James Darren's career in front of the camera began to evolve, so too did his ambitions within the industry. The decision to transition from acting to directing was a significant one, motivated by a desire to expand his creative horizons and take greater control over the stories he was involved in telling. For Darren, directing offered a new set of challenges and opportunities that reignited his passion for the entertainment industry.

The transition was not without its difficulties. Hollywood has long been known for its rigid roles, and actors who attempt to move into directing often face skepticism. Darren had to navigate these challenges while simultaneously learning the intricacies of directing—a craft that required a different set of skills than acting. His early directorial efforts were marked by a steep learning curve, as he worked to understand the technical and creative aspects of guiding a production from behind the camera.

One of the key challenges Darren faced was overcoming the stereotypes that often accompany actors who shift to directing. There was a tendency in Hollywood to view actor-directors as dilettantes, not fully committed to the craft of directing. Darren was determined to prove that he was serious about this new phase of his career. He approached each project with the same dedication and attention to detail that had characterized his acting work, gradually earning the respect of his peers in the industry.

Key Directorial Projects

Darren's first major opportunity as a director came on the set of *T.J. Hooker*, a show in which he was already a key player as an actor. Moving from in front of the camera to behind it allowed Darren to leverage his deep understanding of the show's characters and storylines, enabling him to bring a unique perspective to his directorial work. His ability to balance these dual roles showcased his versatility and his deep commitment to the craft of storytelling.

Following his success on *T.J. Hooker*, Darren went on to direct episodes of some of the most popular television shows of the 1990s, including *Beverly Hills, 90210* and *Melrose Place*. These shows were cultural touchstones of the era, and Darren's work as a director helped shape their iconic status. On these sets, he honed his directorial style, developing a keen eye for character development and pacing, while also managing the complexities of large ensemble casts.

Darren's experience as an actor gave him a unique advantage as a director. He had an intuitive understanding of what actors needed from a director and was able to communicate his vision in a way that resonated with his peers. This empathy and insight were key to his success behind the camera, as they allowed him to create an environment where actors could thrive and deliver their best performances.

Balancing Acting and Directing

Balancing the demands of acting and directing on the same project presented unique challenges. On the one hand, Darren's dual roles allowed him to maintain a cohesive vision for the episodes he worked on. On the other hand, it required an immense amount of focus and energy to switch between the two roles, often within the same day. The experience of directing himself while also managing the broader needs of the production tested Darren's limits, but it also provided a profound sense of accomplishment.

One of the key rewards of this dual role was the ability to maintain artistic integrity across both aspects of his work. As both an actor and a director, Darren could ensure that his portrayal of a character was in line with the overall tone and direction of the episode. This synergy between his acting and directing roles allowed for a more seamless and coherent final product, something that both he and the audiences could appreciate.

Reflecting on his directorial career, Darren recognized that not every project would be a success. There were episodes that didn't resonate as he had hoped, and decisions that, in hindsight, he might have approached differently. However, he viewed these experiences as valuable lessons that informed his growth as a director. The balance between success and failure was a delicate one, but it was integral to his journey in mastering the craft of directing.

Legacy as a Director

James Darren's contributions to television directing have left a lasting impact on the industry. His work on shows like *T.J. Hooker*, *Beverly Hills, 90210*, and *Melrose Place* not only helped define the visual and narrative style of these series but also influenced the next generation of television directors. Darren's ability to seamlessly transition from acting to directing set a precedent, proving that with dedication and talent, it was possible to excel in both roles.

Darren's legacy as a director is also reflected in the way he approached his work with younger, less experienced directors. He was known for being generous with his time and knowledge, often mentoring aspiring directors and actors who were looking to make a similar transition.

His willingness to share his expertise helped to cultivate a culture of collaboration and mutual respect on the sets he worked on, fostering an environment where creativity could flourish.

In the broader context of Hollywood, Darren's career serves as a testament to the power of versatility and adaptability. His successful pivot from acting to directing has inspired many others in the industry to pursue their passions beyond the roles they are initially known for. Darren's contributions to television directing have ensured that his influence will be felt for years to come, solidifying his place as a significant figure in the history of television.

The Music Man

A Successful Music Career

James Darren's entry into the world of music was as seamless as it was successful. While many knew him first as an actor, his musical talents quickly became undeniable with the release of his breakthrough hit, "Goodbye Cruel World." This 1961 single, which soared to the top of the charts, marked the beginning of a flourishing career in music that would see Darren explore a variety of genres and collaborate with some of the most talented musicians of his time.

"Goodbye Cruel World" was a quintessential example of the early 1960s pop sound, combining catchy melodies with Darren's smooth, heartfelt vocals. The song's success was not just a testament to his vocal talent but also to his ability to connect with audiences on an emotional level. This connection became a hallmark of Darren's music, earning him a dedicated fanbase that extended beyond his acting career.

Throughout the 1960s, Darren continued to release a series of successful singles and albums. He was not content to rest on his laurels, instead opting to explore different musical genres, from pop to jazz to swing. His versatility as a singer allowed him to experiment with various sounds and styles, each time bringing his unique touch to the music. Key albums like *The James Darren Sings for All Sizes* showcased his range and ability to adapt to the evolving music scene.

Collaborations with other artists and producers played a significant role in Darren's musical career. He worked with some of the era's most notable figures, including songwriters and arrangers who helped craft the distinctive sound of his records. These collaborations enriched his music, adding layers of complexity and sophistication that resonated with his audience. Each album was a reflection of Darren's growth as an artist, as he continually sought to refine and perfect his craft.

The Sound of the 1960s

As a musician in the 1960s, James Darren became an integral part of the soundtrack of an era defined by rapid cultural change. His music, characterized by its blend of pop sensibilities and emotional depth, captured the spirit of the times while also offering a sense of continuity amidst the social upheaval. Darren's songs provided comfort and joy to a generation that was navigating the complexities of the post-war world.

The influence of Darren's music on pop culture during this period cannot be overstated. His songs were a staple on the radio, and his albums sold in large numbers, making him a household name not just as an actor, but as a bona fide music star. His ability to convey emotion through his voice made his music particularly resonant with listeners, many of whom found solace and inspiration in his lyrics.

Tours and live performances were a crucial aspect of Darren's music career. He had a natural stage presence that endeared him to audiences across the country and beyond.

Whether performing in intimate venues or large concert halls, Darren brought energy and authenticity to each show, making every performance a memorable experience for his fans. These tours allowed him to connect with his audience on a personal level, reinforcing the bond that had been formed through his recordings.

The 1960s were a time of great change in the music industry, with new genres emerging and traditional sounds evolving. Darren adapted to these changes with ease, incorporating elements of the new music scene into his own work while staying true to the style that had made him famous. This ability to grow and evolve as an artist ensured that he remained relevant throughout the decade, continuing to captivate listeners even as musical tastes shifted.

Reviving the Classics

As time went on, James Darren found that there was a growing appetite for nostalgia among his fans and a new generation of listeners. The music of the 1960s had become emblematic of a bygone era, and Darren's classic hits were once again in demand. Recognizing this, Darren embraced the opportunity to revisit his earlier work, breathing new life into the songs that had made him a star.

The appeal of nostalgia was evident in Darren's later albums and performances, where he often revisited his old hits, giving them a fresh twist while retaining the elements that had originally made them popular. These performances were not just a trip down memory lane but a celebration of a career that had stood the test of time. Darren's voice, still as captivating as ever, brought these classics to life for both old fans and new listeners alike.

In addition to performing his old hits, Darren continued to produce new music, proving that his creative spark was far from extinguished. His later albums, while often steeped in the nostalgic sound of the past, also incorporated contemporary influences, showcasing his ability to adapt to the times without losing his musical identity. These works were a testament to

Darren's enduring talent and his commitment to his craft.

Music remained a central part of Darren's life well into his later years. Even as he took on new roles in acting and directing, he never strayed far from his musical roots. For Darren, music was more than just a career; it was a lifelong passion that brought him joy and fulfillment. His enduring voice, both as a singer and as a cultural icon, ensured that his legacy in music would continue to resonate with audiences for generations to come.

Vic Fontaine's Musical Legacy

In 1998, James Darren was introduced to a new generation of fans through his role as Vic Fontaine on *Star Trek: Deep Space Nine*. This character, a holographic lounge singer, became an iconic figure in the *Star Trek* universe, thanks in no small part to Darren's portrayal. As Vic Fontaine, Darren brought his love of jazz and swing to the small screen, introducing these classic genres to a new audience.

Vic Fontaine was more than just a character; he was a reflection of Darren's own musical passions. The role allowed Darren to indulge in his love of jazz standards, performing songs that were close to his heart. The character's charm and wit, combined with Darren's smooth vocals, made Vic Fontaine a fan favorite, and his musical performances became some of the most memorable moments on the show.

The influence of Vic Fontaine extended beyond the confines of the *Star Trek* series. Darren's performances as Fontaine brought renewed attention to the genres of jazz and swing, sparking interest among viewers who may not have been familiar with these styles of music. Darren's portrayal of Fontaine was a reminder of the timeless appeal of these genres, and his performances resonated with both old fans and new.

Even after *Deep Space Nine* ended, Darren continued to perform as Vic Fontaine at various events and conventions, delighting fans with live renditions of the songs that had become synonymous with the character. This ongoing connection to Fontaine allowed Darren to keep his music alive in a way that was both nostalgic and forward-looking, ensuring that his voice would continue to be heard long after the show had ended.

Darren's enduring voice, whether as himself or as Vic Fontaine, has left an indelible mark on the world of music. His ability to bridge the gap between past and present, between nostalgia and innovation, has ensured that his musical legacy will continue to inspire and entertain for years to come.

Behind the Scenes

The Hollywood Experience

James Darren's career in Hollywood was marked by a series of significant collaborations that shaped his trajectory in the entertainment industry. Working with renowned actors such as Sandra Dee and Cliff Robertson provided Darren with invaluable experience and insights into the world of film. His role as Moondoggie in *Gidget* opposite Sandra Dee was a defining moment in his career, helping to establish him as a teen idol. The chemistry between Darren and Dee was palpable, and their performances were instrumental in the film's success.

Relationships with co-stars and directors were crucial to Darren's career. His ability to forge strong professional relationships and navigate the often-complex dynamics of a film set contributed to his longevity in the industry. Darren's rapport with directors and fellow actors was marked by mutual respect and collaboration. His professionalism and dedication earned him admiration from those he worked with, helping to build a reputation as a reliable and talented performer.

Navigating the studio system was another challenge Darren faced. During the height of his career, the studio system was a dominant force in Hollywood, with studios exerting considerable control over actors' careers. Darren managed to maneuver through this system with a combination of talent, perseverance, and strategic choices. His ability to adapt and remain relevant despite the changing dynamics of the industry is a testament to his skill and resilience.

Anecdotes and Stories

The world of Hollywood is often as intriguing behind the scenes as it is on screen. Darren's time on set was filled with memorable moments that have become part of his legacy. From humorous on-set incidents to dramatic behind-the-scenes stories, these anecdotes provide a glimpse into the life of a man who was as captivating off-screen as he was on it.

One notable anecdote involves a particularly challenging scene during the filming of *Gidget*. The production faced unexpected weather conditions, which created obstacles for the crew and cast. Darren's ability to remain calm under pressure and find creative solutions helped salvage the scene and contributed to the film's successful completion. Such stories highlight Darren's professionalism and adaptability, qualities that were instrumental in his successful career.

Challenges and triumphs in filming were part and parcel of Darren's career. Whether it was dealing with difficult production schedules or overcoming personal doubts, Darren's experiences on set were a mix of highs and lows. His resilience in the face of adversity and his ability to celebrate victories, both big and small, reflect his commitment to his craft and his passion for storytelling.

Lessons learned in the industry were numerous for Darren. From the importance of preparation and collaboration to the value of perseverance, his experiences provided him with a wealth of knowledge that he carried throughout his career. These lessons not only shaped his professional life but also influenced his approach to personal challenges and relationships.

Personal Life and Relationships

Balancing personal and professional life was a delicate endeavor for James Darren. His marriage and family life were central to his well-being and happiness, providing a source of support and stability amidst the demands of a high-profile career. Darren's dedication to his family was evident in his efforts to maintain a strong presence at home, despite the often-grueling schedules of his professional life.

Friends and colleagues played a significant role in Darren's personal life. The bonds he formed with fellow actors, directors, and industry professionals were more than just professional relationships; they were genuine friendships that provided him with a network of support. These lasting connections were a testament to Darren's character and his ability to build meaningful relationships in an industry known for its fleeting associations.

Coping with fame and privacy was a challenge that Darren navigated with grace. The intense scrutiny and public attention that came with his career could be overwhelming, but Darren managed to maintain a sense of normalcy in his personal life. He approached the pressures of fame with a balanced perspective, finding ways to protect his privacy while still engaging with his fans and the public.

Insights from Close Associates

Insights from family, friends, and co-stars provide a deeper understanding of James Darren as a person. Interviews and reflections from those who knew him best offer valuable perspectives on his character and contributions to the entertainment industry. These personal accounts help paint a more complete picture of Darren, beyond the public persona.

Recollections of working with Darren reveal the respect and admiration he garnered from those around him. Colleagues often speak of his professionalism, kindness, and dedication, highlighting the positive impact he had on set. These stories serve as a testament to Darren's influence and the regard in which he was held by his peers.

The man behind the roles was a complex and multifaceted individual. Personal reflections from those closest to Darren provide insights into his motivations, values, and passions. These perspectives offer a glimpse into the private life of a man who was beloved by many and whose legacy continues to resonate in the world of entertainment.

The Legacy of James Darren

A Lasting Impact on Film and Television

James Darren's contributions to film and television have left an indelible mark on the entertainment industry. His influence on surf culture through his iconic role as Moondoggie in *Gidget* helped shape the way surf culture was portrayed in the media. The film, which captured the carefree and adventurous spirit of the surfing lifestyle, resonated with audiences and became a cultural touchstone. Darren's portrayal of Moondoggie contributed to the film's enduring popularity and cemented his place in the annals of pop culture.

In television, Darren's career spanned several decades, showcasing his versatility and adaptability as an actor. His roles in shows like *The Time Tunnel*, *T.J. Hooker*, and *Star Trek: Deep Space Nine* demonstrated his ability to navigate different genres and formats. Each role added a unique dimension to his career, from the adventurous time-traveling hero to the charismatic Vic Fontaine, the holographic lounge singer. Darren's contributions to television reflect his broad appeal and his impact on the medium.

Darren's status as a cultural icon was reinforced by his diverse body of work. His roles in film and television, coupled with his musical achievements, made him a multi-faceted performer whose influence extended beyond any single genre. His ability to connect with audiences across different platforms and eras is a testament to his enduring legacy in the entertainment industry.

Music and Beyond

James Darren's place in the music industry is marked by a series of notable achievements that defined his career. His success with hits like "Goodbye Cruel World" established him as a prominent figure in the 1960s music scene. Darren's contributions to music were not limited to his chart-topping singles; his albums and performances showcased his versatility as an artist and his ability to adapt to changing musical trends.

Darren's influence on future generations of musicians is evident in the way his music has been remembered and celebrated. His ability to blend pop, jazz, and swing created a distinctive sound that continues to inspire artists. The quality of his recordings and the depth of his musical expression have served as a model for musicians who value both technical skill and emotional connection in their work.

The continuing popularity of Darren's music is a testament to his lasting appeal. Even decades after his peak in the music industry, his songs remain beloved by fans and are often revisited by new audiences. The nostalgia associated with his music, combined with its inherent quality, ensures that his legacy in the music world endures.

Fans and Fandom

James Darren's fans and fandom were integral to his career and legacy. The cult following of characters like Moondoggie and Vic Fontaine highlights the impact Darren had on his audience. Fans embraced his roles with enthusiasm, creating a lasting connection that transcended the screen. This dedicated fan base contributed to the ongoing popularity of Darren's work and his status as a beloved figure in entertainment.

Interactions with fans were an important aspect of Darren's career. He made numerous public appearances and attended conventions, where he engaged with his audience and expressed his appreciation for their support. These interactions allowed fans to connect with Darren on a personal level, reinforcing their admiration and loyalty.

Darren's role in fan communities was more than just a byproduct of his career; it was an active engagement that demonstrated his appreciation for his supporters. His involvement in fan events and his willingness to share his experiences with his audience helped build a strong and enduring connection between him and his fans.

The Final Years

Reflections on James Darren's storied career reveal a life filled with achievements and contributions to the entertainment industry. His final years were marked by a deep sense of accomplishment and a continued connection to his fans and the industry he loved. Darren's reflections on his career highlight the satisfaction and pride he took in his work and the impact he had on those who knew and admired him.

His health and final days were a period of personal and professional reflection. Despite facing health challenges, Darren remained active and engaged with his work and his fans. His ability to maintain his passion and dedication even in his later years is a testament to his resilience and love for his craft.

Conclusion

Reflecting on a Remarkable Career

James Darren's career trajectory is a testament to his versatility and enduring appeal. Starting as a teen idol in the 1950s with his iconic role as Moondoggie in *Gidget*, Darren transitioned seamlessly into a seasoned industry veteran, making notable contributions to both film and television. His evolution from a youthful heartthrob to a respected actor, director, and musician exemplifies the breadth of his talent and dedication to his craft.

Key lessons from Darren's life include the importance of adaptability and perseverance. Throughout his career, Darren demonstrated an ability to reinvent himself, from navigating typecasting to embracing new roles and opportunities. His journey underscores the value of maintaining passion and resilience in the face of challenges, both personal and professional.

The dual legacies of Darren in film and music highlight the breadth of his influence. His work in television and film, coupled with his successful music career, showcases his multifaceted talents and the diverse ways in which he connected with audiences. Darren's ability to excel in both domains solidifies his status as a remarkable and influential figure in entertainment.

Darren's Place in Hollywood History

James Darren's place in Hollywood history is marked by his significant contributions across multiple genres and decades. His roles in classic films and television shows helped shape the landscape of entertainment during the Golden Age and beyond. Darren's work with esteemed directors and actors, coupled with his innovative approach to both acting and directing, has earned him a lasting legacy in Hollywood.

In comparing Darren with his contemporaries, it becomes clear that his versatility set him apart. While many actors of his era specialized in particular genres, Darren's ability to traverse between teen idol roles, dramatic parts, and comedic performances made him a standout. His unique blend of talent and charisma ensured that he left a distinct mark on the industry.

Contributions to the Golden Age of Hollywood are evident in Darren's involvement in iconic productions and collaborations. His work helped define a generation of entertainment, and his influence is still felt in modern media. Darren's ability to blend with the evolving trends of Hollywood while maintaining his unique style contributed to his enduring impact on the industry.

The Enduring Influence

James Darren's legacy continues to resonate in modern pop culture. His roles in *Gidget*, *Star Trek: Deep Space Nine*, and his music have left an indelible mark on entertainment. Darren's influence extends beyond his era, as his work continues to be celebrated and revisited by new generations of fans and creators.

The inspiration Darren provides is reflected in the admiration he receives from both peers and admirers. His dedication to his craft and his ability to connect with audiences serve as a model for aspiring actors, musicians, and filmmakers. Darren's career offers valuable lessons in perseverance, passion, and creativity.

Future generations will view Darren's work with appreciation for its historical significance and its contribution to the entertainment industry. His legacy will be remembered not only for his accomplishments but also for the way he impacted those who experienced his work. The continued celebration of his contributions ensures that his influence will persist in shaping the future of entertainment.

Final Thoughts

Summing up the impact of James Darren involves recognizing the breadth and depth of his contributions to film, television, and music. His career reflects a dedication to his craft and an ability to connect with audiences across multiple platforms. Darren's legacy is a testament to his talent, resilience, and enduring appeal.

The personal significance of writing this book lies in the opportunity to honor a legend whose work has touched many lives. By exploring Darren's career, contributions, and influence, this book aims to provide a comprehensive tribute to a remarkable individual whose impact on entertainment continues to be felt.

A tribute to James Darren acknowledges not only his professional achievements but also the personal qualities that endeared him to those who knew him. His legacy, marked by his diverse talents and lasting influence, ensures that he will be remembered as a significant and cherished figure in the history of entertainment.